# Your Heart

## Melvin and Gilda Berger

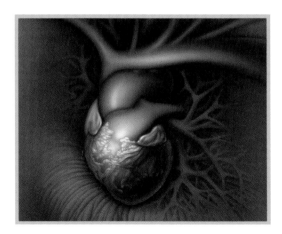

**SCHOLASTIC INC.**
New York  Toronto  London  Auckland  Sydney
Mexico City  New Delhi  Hong Kong  Buenos Aires

Photographs: Cover: © Dorling Kindersley; p. 1: Custom Medical Stock Photo;
p. 3: Rubberball Productions/PictureQuest; p. 4: Custom Medical Stock Photo;
p. 5: Scott Bodell/PictureQuest/Photodisc; p. 6: Dorling Kindersley/Getty Images;
p. 7: Scott Bodell/PictureQuest/Photodisc;
p. 8: MACHET B2M/PictureQuest; p. 9: © Mark Richards/PhotoEdit;
p. 10: Getty Images/Beateworks; p: 11: PictureQuest/Digital Vision;
p. 12: Custom Medical Stock Photo; p. 13: © Christina Kennedy/PhotoEdit;
p. 14: PictureQuest/Creatas; p. 15: PictureQuest/Corbis;
p. 16: © Michael Newman/PhotoEdit.

Photo Research: Sarah Longacre/Dwayne Howard

ISBN 0-439-77369-5

12 11 10 9 8 7 6 5 4 3 2 1                    5 6 7 8 9 10/0

Printed in the U.S.A.
First printing, September 2005

What does your heart do?

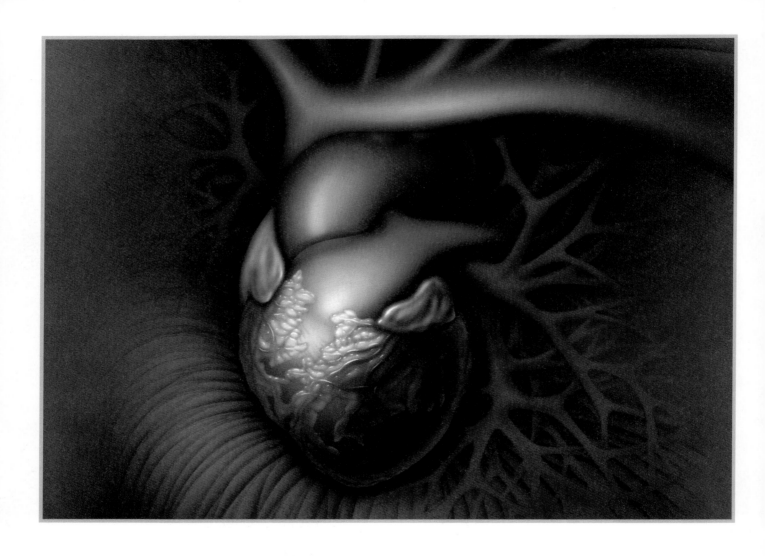

Your heart pumps blood.

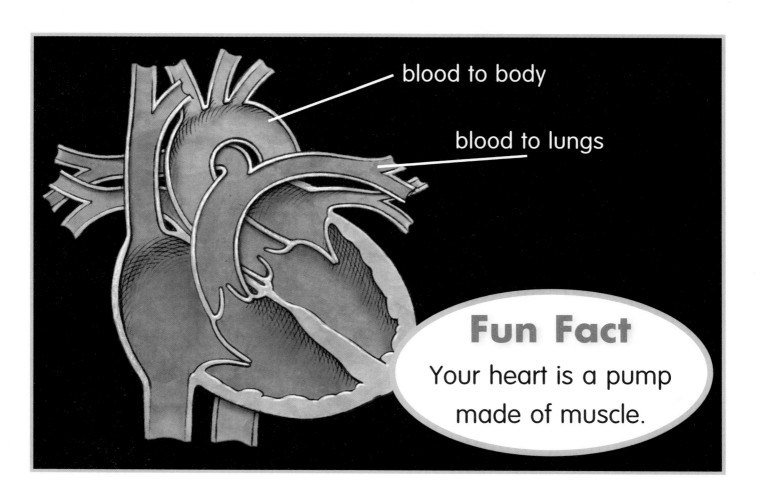

The blood goes out
from your heart.

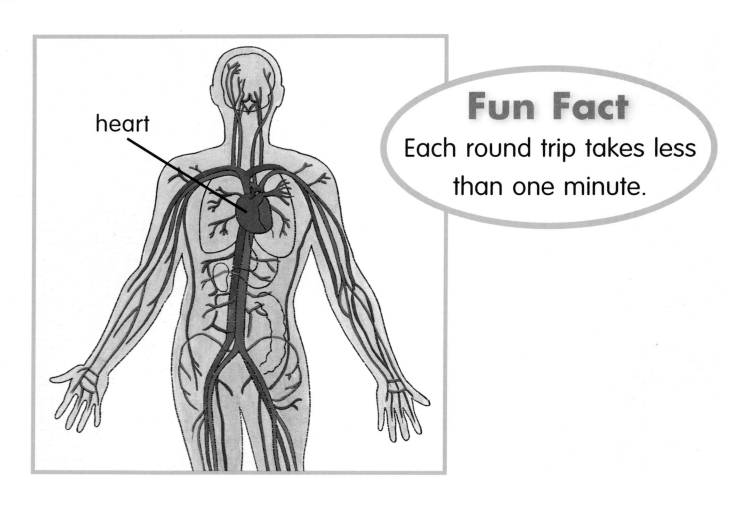

heart

The blood goes to every part of your body.

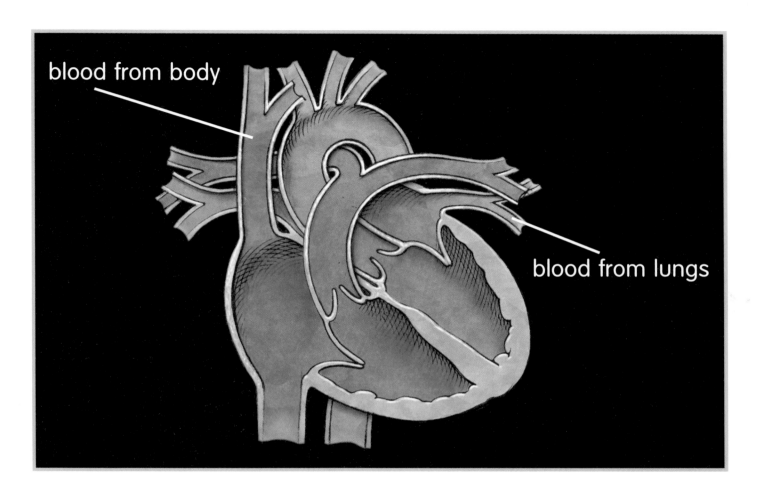

blood from body

blood from lungs

The blood flows back
to your heart.

**Fun Fact**

Kids' hearts beat faster than the hearts of grown-ups.

Your heart beats all day.

It beats faster
when you play.

Your heart beats slowly when you rest.

**Fun Fact**

The beating of your heart is called your pulse.

Your heart beats even more slowly when you sleep.

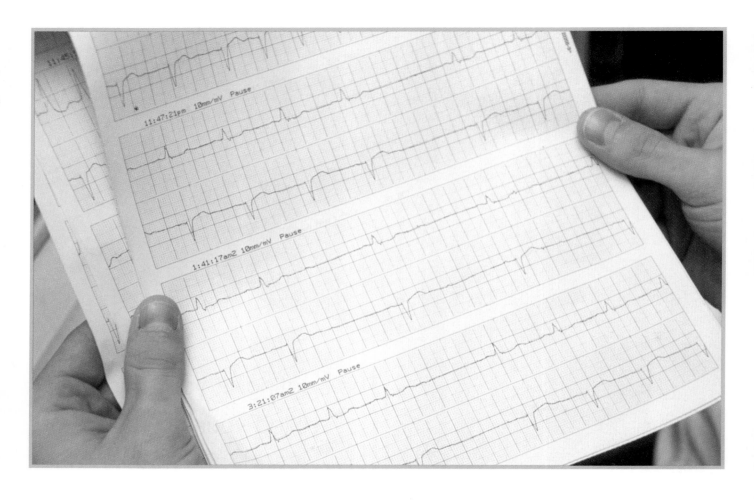

Each pump of your heart
is one heartbeat.

You can feel your heartbeat.

Fun Fact

The heartbeat tells the
doctor if the heart is
healthy or not.

A doctor can hear
your heartbeat.

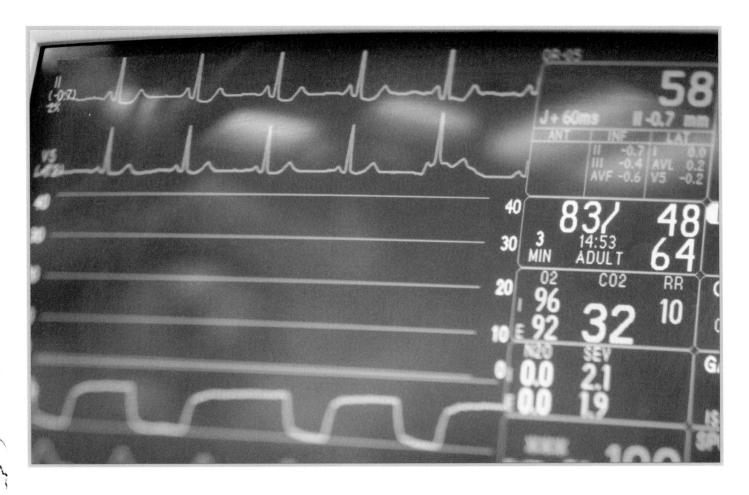

A doctor can see your
heartbeat, too.

You can hear a friend's heartbeat.